CONCERT REPERTOIRE FOR
CLARINET
with piano

edited, selected and arranged by
ausgewählt, herausgegeben und bearbeitet von
choisi, édité et arrangé par

Paul Harris
&
Emma Johnson

FABER *ff* MUSIC

© 2003 by Faber Music Ltd
First published in 2003 by Faber Music Ltd
3 Queen Square London WC1N 3AU
Cover illustration by Drew Hillier
Cover design by Nick Flower
Music processed by Jackie Leigh
Printed in England by Caligraving Ltd

ISBN 0-571-52166-5

To buy Faber Music publications or to find out about the full range of titles available
please contact your local music retailer or Faber Music sales enquiries:

Faber Music Limited, Burnt Mill, Elizabeth Way, Harlow, CM20 2HX England
Tel: +44 (0)1279 82 89 82   Fax: +44 (0)1279 82 89 83
sales@fabermusic.com   fabermusic.com

CONTENTS

The force of destiny

Giuseppe Verdi
(1813–1901)

Bring me, said David, the harp I adore,
I long ere death calls me, to play it once more.

David of the white rock

Traditional Welsh folksong

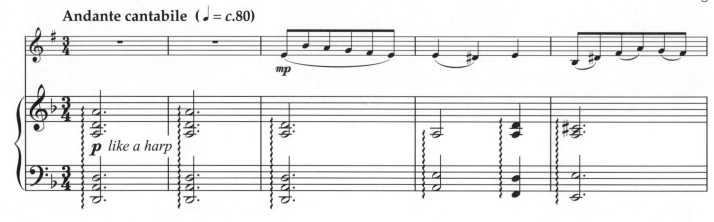

Policemen's Dance

from *Sweeney Todd*

Malcolm Arnold

Caprice at Corfu

Hyacinthe Klosé
(1808–1880)

Silent movie

Paul Harris

* For F trill use the G sharp key.

Tarantella

Heinrich Joseph Baermann
(1784–1847)

D.S. 𝄉 al Fine

Ragtime Dance

Scott Joplin
(1868–1917)

E lucevan le stelle

from *Tosca*

Giacomo Puccini
(1858–1924)

Andante cantabile

No.2 from *Three Miniatures*

Krzysztof Penderecki

I got rhythm

George Gershwin (1898–1937)
and Ira Gershwin (1896–1983)

Swung, alla Benny Goodman

Gut reaction

Paul Harris

Larghetto
2nd movement from Clarinet Quintet

Wolfgang Amadeus Mozart
(1756–1791)

D.C. al 𝄌 poi al Coda

CODA

Vivace ma non troppo

2nd movement from Sonata Op.49 No.1 in A♭

Max Reger
(1873–1916)

Vivace ma non troppo (♩. = 72)

Bach goes to town

Alec Templeton
(1909–1963)